G-4391
$7.95

COME ALL YOU PEOPLE

Shorter songs for worship

from the Iona Community

John L. Bell
and the
Wild Goose Worship Group

GIA Publications, Inc.
Chicago

GIA Publications, Inc.
7404 S. Mason Ave.
Chicago, IL 60638
U.S.A.
(708) 496-3800

Design and illustration by Graham Maule
Music origination by Jeanne Fisher, Ludlow, Shrops

CONTENTS

INTRODUCTION

Shorter Songs have a long pedigree in Scotland, as they have elsewhere.

Many of us learned some in our early years in the Church. They were called choruses. They rarely had any more than one verse and they were usually associated with a positive-sounding text such as:

Running over, running over,
my cup's full and running over.
Since the Lord saved me,
I'm as happy as can be;
my cup's full and running over.

or, more simply:

I am H.A.P.P.Y.
I am H.A.P.P.Y.
I know I am, I'm sure I am,
I am H.A.P.P.Y.

People who were not exposed in infancy to chorus books may have learned another kind of shorter song in church:

Thank you for the world so sweet,
thank you for the food we eat,
thank you for the birds that sing,
thank you God, for everything.

or:

Praise God from whom all blessings flow;
praise him all creatures here below;
praise him above ye heavenly host;
praise Father, Son and Holy Ghost.

This latter type was not intended to reflect the state of the soul so much as to let action happen. After singing the above, the chances are that food would be served.

Then there were songs such as:

> Jesus loves me! This I know
> for the Bible tells me so.

Again, a different intention is behind the song. It is reflecting a biblical or theological truth. These songs (like contemporary choruses such as *A new commandment I give unto you*) often are direct quotations from scripture or simple paraphrases set to music.

Then, depending on whether you were brought up as a Roman Catholic, an Anglican, a Methodist or a Presbyterian, you may have sung in church other shorter songs such as:

> *Kyrie eleison, Christe eleison* (Lord have mercy, Christ have mercy)

or:

> Holy, Holy, Holy,
> Lord God of Hosts,
> Heaven and earth are full of your glory.
> Hosanna in the highest!

or:

> The Lord bless thee and keep thee,
> the Lord make his face to shine upon thee
> and be gracious unto thee.
> The Lord lift up his countenance upon thee
> and give thee peace.

or simply:

> Amen. Amen. Amen.

These shorter songs were to enable the liturgy or order of worship to progress.

And we remember such items, partly because of their length, partly because – as with *The Lord bless thee* – they may have accompanied important ceremonies like baptism, and partly because they rang true in our young minds and may still ring true today.

One of the most important ecumenical phenomena of the 20th century, the Taizé Community, has been responsible for promoting its own variety of shorter songs, often referred to as Taizé chants. Some of them fulfil one of the above functions; some are sung repeatedly as an aid to meditation or prayer.

The songs in this collection may seem to bear closest resemblance to Taizé's variety, but actually their roots are very different. They draw on three sources of inspiration.

1 The ancient Scottish practice of singing simple harmonized songs for worship, one of the oldest of which can be found as the first *Gloria* in the Acclamation section.

2 The plethora of verse songs, many with complex harmony lines from the indigenous churches of Southern Africa, and more simple harmonized liturgical responses found in traditions as far apart as the Russian Orthodox Church and Latin American charismatic assemblies.

3 The songs of childhood, as illustrated above.

The temptation to call these songs 'chants' has been resisted, simply because that word has denominational overtones which may be sweet or sour depending on your tradition. Hence 'shorter songs'.

In our work throughout Britain over the past ten years, these songs have been invaluable. They have been a godsend with a congregation or audience of 200 when the song sheets only numbered 50. No need to read the words if you can quickly memorize them! They have been of tremendous advantage in enabling people to move in worship, whether to light a candle, present an offering or move out of the church together. Such things can't happen easily if worshippers are clutching a book. (Try lighting a candle with one hand while holding the words for *Abide with me* in the other.) They have provided music for worship which has managed to transcend the *Hymns-Ancient-and-Modern/Mission-Praise* divide and have been sung both by cathedral choirs and unkempt teenagers.

They have also enabled people who believed they couldn't sing to catch hold of and keep a harmony line – whether that be the simple pentatonic Amen with which the book ends or, as numerous Greenbelt Festival-goers will attest, the more complex but highly enjoyable songs such as *Behold the Lamb of God (2)* or *From the rising of the sun*.

Apart from being comprised solely of shorter songs, two things make this publication distinctive:

1 There are no special keyboard parts or guitar chords.

   Of course, the songs can be accompanied with a keyboard playing the harmony lines, but none of the songs began their life in that way. And because they were meant primarily for voices a capella, the harmony changes too frequently for many of them to sit happily with a guitar accompaniment. A flute, fiddle or drum might prove much more appropriate.

2 While most of the songs here are original, there are two that come from the historic Church and four that come from the World Church.

   It has been important for our work not to be isolated in a musical ghetto of our own making, but to recognize and draw on other traditions, particularly those of the Third World churches. We have already published two books of World Church songs, and we have listed appropriate material from them and from other collections at the end of each section.

If you are interested in seeing liturgical material, especially corporate prayer, that makes use of shorter songs included in this collection, have a look at *A Wee Worship Book* (see page 95).

We offer this book with the hope that the songs and suggestions for their use may enliven both the minds and the worship of God's people.

John L Bell
and the Wild Goose Worship Group
The Iona Community
840 Govan Road
Glasgow G51 3UU
Scotland

DEADLY THREATS
AND SOLEMN WARNINGS

1   DO NOT sit down at the piano with this book and go through it from front to back unless that is the way you read dictionaries and telephone directories.

2   In fact, DO NOT sit down at the piano with it. Sing everything out loud until the neighbours complain. Then ask them in to take the alto and bass parts.

3   DO NOT object that your neighbours cannot sing. DO NOT even object that your congregation cannot sing, unless medical certification regarding anatomical abnormalities is available. Everybody can sing. It just happens that one in four believe they can't, usually because of the friendly advice of a parent, teacher, boyfriend or girlfriend during a delicate stage of development.

4   Conceding that everyone can sing, DO NOT then argue that not everyone can sing in parts. It happens in nearly every country in the southern hemisphere and it used to happen in Britain until music changed from a participative activity to a spectator sport.

5   DO NOT then go on about 'reading music'. All the melody lines of these songs have been taught without music, and a surprising number of the harmony lines have similarly been taught. It is quite possible to get through half the songs in this book and have the congregation singing them in parts with only one copy, i.e. this one. How's that for a bargain from Scotland!

6   DO NOT think that this book is just for the choir. But DO NOT think that this book is *not* for the choir. There are a number of introits lurking under different guises in these pages. There are also a number of responsive

songs for use in prayer which come alive when the congregation sings the tune and the choir supplies the harmony.

7 DO NOT dismiss this book as being full of 'Catholic Chants' or 'Protestant Choruses'. It is full of neither. Read the Introduction (which is much more polite than this bit).

8 DO NOT sing some of these songs 53 times à la Taizé and then wonder why people are not responding. Given the difference in temperature between Taizé and Tarbert, singers in the latter region may have succumbed to hypothermia at the 28th singing. These songs are not just for people who are 'into' meditation.

9 DO NOT imagine that these songs were written by the monks on Iona. There have been no monks on Iona for over 400 years. And though these songs are sung in the Abbey on Iona, they originated in an overcrowded living room next to one of the most heavily polluted arterial roads in Glasgow. Anyone who can hear the waves lapping on the Sound of Mull when singing these songs should be referred to a specialist.

10 DO NOT, after reading the above, become so incensed that you decide to return this book to the shop where you purchased it and write a letter of complaint to the publishers. The shop has just gone into receivership and the publishers consist of two short-sighted pensioners who take turns to crank out sheets from a manually operated duplicator.

GATHERING

When Christians gather for worship, they do not require to be in a special building at a special time. Jesus promised to be present wherever his people came together in his name.

The gathering together is therefore the identification of a particular group of people as both an assembly for God and a community in which all present belong. One of the aspects of this gathering which makes evident its intention is the song of the people. In it they both address God and bond themselves to each other.

In many non-Western cultures, where the weather is more predictable or where there are no consecrated buildings, a gathering song is what signals the beginning of the worship service.

COME ALL YOU PEOPLE (Uyai mose) is such a song. It has a very simple tune which should be sung by women, a similar line for half the men and a lower sequence of notes for the other half. There is also a more elaborate cantor's part which can be sung solo or by a group of sopranos.

Do not shrink from what looks like complexity. This song has been taught to crowds of hundreds, all over Britain, without any of the singers ever seeing the music. All it requires is for three people to demonstrate the three main lines. A female should sing the tune and get all other women to join her. One man then teaches the second line to half of the males in the congregation, a second male teaches the lowest part and then in succeeding verses the parts join in one at a time. When everyone is singing, the cantor's descant can be added, most effectively by a singer or singers at the back of the assembly.

Uyai mose comes from Zimbabwe. It has been harmonized along traditional lines. The word 'Ahom' sung by the men is simply the kind of sound without clear meaning which is common to folk music throughout the world. In Britain, the equivalent might be 'la la la'.

COME, HOLY SPIRIT is an invocation of the Spirit as distinct from a summons to the people. It simply requires the congregation to repeat the cantor's line, holding on to the last note of each phrase. It can be sung extremely quietly or with great power, depending on the occasion. As with *Uyai mose*, it does not require the cantor to stand in front; it can just as easily be led from the rear. *Maranatha* is an Aramaic word meaning, 'Come quickly, Lord'.

COME, HOLY SPIRIT, DESCEND ON US is a prayer for the presence of the Spirit within the act of worship. The cantor leads from one singing to another by addressing the Spirit by different names. Circumstances will dictate which of the modes of address are appropriate and more can be employed *ad hoc*. For this song to work best, a choir singing in harmony should accompany the congregation singing in unison.

HEAVEN AND EARTH. This song, which stands in an ancient tradition of linking the worship of the Church on earth to that of the universe and the Church in heaven, has a number of uses.

It can be used simple to call people to worship as a kind of gathering song. It can be used as an affirmation after the reading of scripture. It can be used as a response during a prayer of gratitude; or it can be used as a recessional.

It is most easily and effectively sung when a cantor sings each line followed by the whole congregation. That way the speed and volume can be altered ad lib.

Other similar songs
(See page 95 for more information on the following publications.)
Be still and know – *Love from Below*
May the words of my mouth – *Psalms of Patience, Protest and Praise*
Yesuve saranam (India) – *Many and Great*
Wa wa wa Emimimo (Nigeria) – *Many and Great*
Maranatha (Philippines) – *Sent by the Lord*
Re ya mathemata (South Africa) – *Sent by the Lord*
Jesu tawa pano (Zimbabwe) – *Many and Great*

Come all you people (Uyai mose)

Tune & words: Alexander Gondo
Arrangement: JLB

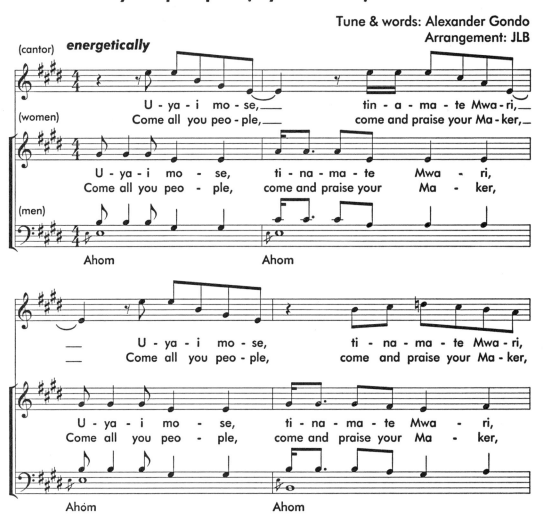

Uyai mose, tinamate Mwari (x3)
Uyai mose zvino.

Come all you people, come and praise your Maker (x3)
Come now and worship the Lord.

15

Come, Holy Spirit

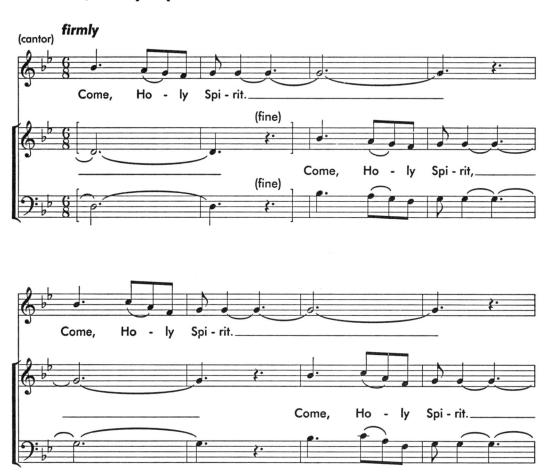

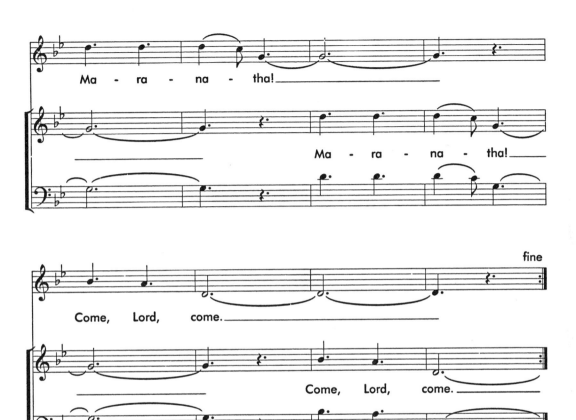

Ma - ra - na - tha!_____

Ma - ra - na - tha!_____

fine

Come, Lord, come._____

Come, Lord, come._____

Come, Holy Spirit.
Come, Holy Spirit.
Maranatha!
Come, Lord, come.

Come, Holy Spirit, descend on us

gently

Come, Ho - ly Spi - rit, de - scend on us, de -

- scend on us. We ga - ther here in Je - sus'

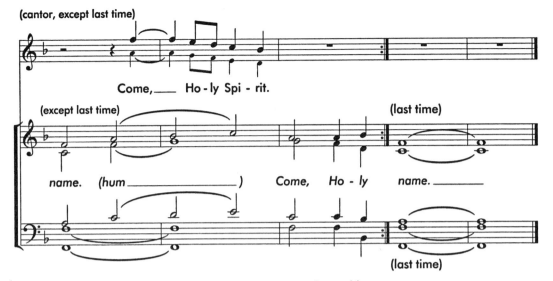

ANTIPHON:

Come, Holy Spirit,
descend on us, descend on us.
We gather here in Jesus' name.

Cantor(s):

1. Come, Holy Spirit.

2. Come, Breath of Heaven,

3. Come, Word of Mercy,

4. Come, Fire of Judgement,

5. Come, Great Creator,

6. Come to unite us.

7. Come to disturb us.

8. Come to inspire us.

(other invocations ad lib.)

Heaven and earth

Hea - ven and earth, join to wor - ship your Cre - a - tor!

Hea - ven and earth, join to wor - ship.

Sing to the Lord, praise the One from whom you came.

Sing to the Lord from whom you came.

Sing a new song to the God who goes be-fore us,

Sing a new song to the God be - fore us,

Hum

ma-king all new, leav-ing no-bo-dy the same.

ma-king all new, leav - ing none the same.

Cantor: Heaven and earth,
        join to worship your Creator!
        Sing to the Lord,
        praise the One from whom you came.
All: (Repeat)

Cantor: Sing a new song
        to the God who goes before us,
        making all new,
        leaving nobody the same.
All: (Repeat)

PRAISE

Praise is the offering of love and adoration which we express to God simply because God is God and is worth praising. Praise does not seek to flatter, to wheedle concessions, to expound theological insights or to express the condition of the worshipper. Praise is for and about God, celebrating the splendour of God's glory and that unmerited goodness which we know as grace.

And because God's grace always precedes our need for it, we sing songs of praise in worship before we confess our sin.

There are several other items in this collection which may rightly be used as praise songs. The three offered here are all different in type, though not in intention.

NOW LET US SING is an adaptation of a 16th century text, Nou lat us sing which featured in a collection called The Gude and Godlie Ballatis, published in Dundee as a first volume of post-reformation congregational song. The tune, possibly folk in origin, has the distinct advantage of being singable as a canon. The original words referred to the Nativity.

LAUDATE OMNES GENTES uses words from Psalm 117 – 'Praise the Lord, all you nations'. The tenor line may be omitted, and the song taught to the congregation in two parts instead of three.

Being so short, this item can be creatively used in a number of ways. One is as an interjection between verses read from a psalm such as Psalm 47 or Psalm 48. The sung response to the Word of God engages people in a dynamic relationship to the text.

Another possibility is to use the song as an acclamation at the beginning of a conference or meeting of people gathered from different parts of the country or world. A particular group may be introduced and then stand while the others sing the Laudate. The process continues until all have been introduced.

It is a much more spirited and spiritual procedure than giving rounds of luke-warm applause.

FROM THE RISING OF THE SUN takes its text from Psalm 113 and its style from African gathering songs such as *Uyai mose*. It is remarkably easy to teach and to sing. Men have simple lines which can be given *ad hoc* to all on the right or the left, all upstairs or downstairs. In a similar fashion, women's voices can be divided in two without distinguishing sopranos from altos. Most people should be able to sing any line.

Once the parts are known, gradually build up the song. Start the lower men's part, add the upper men's part, then the women who sing the longer text and finally those who exclaim 'Praise the Lord'.

Once a congregation or choir is familiar with the song, it may be used as an interjecting response in the same way as *Laudate omnes gentes* above.

Other similar songs
(See page 95 for more information on the following publications.)
Magnificat – *Heaven shall not Wait*
Cantai ao Senhor (Brazil) – *Sent by the Lord*
Bayavuya (South Africa) – *Sent by the Lord*

Now let us sing

Tune: traditional
Words: traditional (adapted JLB)

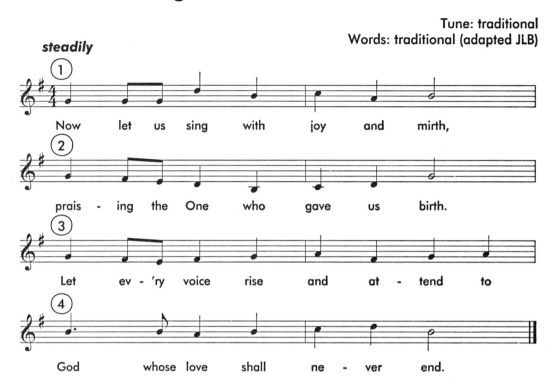

Now let us sing with joy and mirth,
praising the One who gave us birth.
Let ev'ry voice rise and attend
to God whose love shall never end.

Laudate omnes gentes

Words: Ps 117

Laudate omnes gentes,
laudate Dominum.

(O Praise God all you nations,
praise the Lord.)

From the rising of the sun

not too quickly

Words: Ps 113.3

(descant)

Praise,_____ praise___ the___

(women)

From the ris - ing of the___ sun and un - til its

(men)

All you who are___ God's ser - vants,

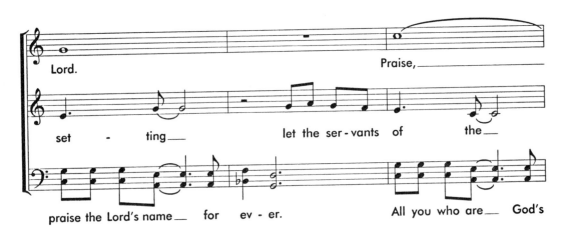

Lord. Praise,_____

set - ting___ let the ser - vants of the___

praise the Lord's name___ for ev - er. All you who are___ God's

praise the Lord. (fine)

Lord praise his ho-ly name (From the ris-ing) *(fine)

ser-vants praise the Lord's name for ev-er. (fine)

* 𝅝 last time

Women
From the rising of the sun
and until its setting,
let the servants of the Lord
praise his holy name.

Men
All ye who are God's servants
praise the Lord's name for ever. (x2)

CONFESSION

The health of any personal relationship depends on the ability of the people concerned to deal effectively with what goes wrong – in other words, to confess and forgive. In the relationship we have with God, both individually and as community, the same applies. We need to be able to admit our wrong, express our regret and believe that we are forgiven.

One way to do this is to ensure that in prayers of confession, the whole congregation, and not only the leader, actively makes expression of repentance. This is an ancient Christian practice. The *Kyrie* has, for over 1500 years been such a shared prayer. In its most classical form, *Kyrie eleison* (Lord have mercy) was said or sung three times. *Christe eleison* (Christ have mercy) was similarly said or sung, followed by the *Kyrie* three times more.

When, therefore, we use these ancient Greek words, we not only identify ourselves with the historical church of Jesus Christ; we share the possibility of forgiveness with countless millions of Christians through the ages.

JESUS CHRIST, SON OF GOD. At its simplest, this can be a single line of music sung once by a cantor then repeated several times by the congregation. This would happen at a specific time during a prayer of confession.

Alternatively, the line could be sung between short statements such as:

Where we have failed to love you, our God, with all our soul and strength and mind

Jesus Christ, Son of God, have mercy upon us

Where we have failed to love our brother, our sister, our neighbour

Jesus Christ, Son of God, have mercy upon us

Where we have failed to love our friends and refused to love our enemies

Jesus Christ, Son of God, have mercy upon us

Where we have failed to love ourselves and neglected your image within us

Jesus Christ, Son of God, have mercy upon us

The harmonized version, with the melody in the bass, may be used when the congregation is familiar with the tune.

KYRIE ELEISON 1. This is a very elementary four-part Kyrie which can be taught as such without need of music. It is best employed in a prayer such as the above.

KYRIE ELEISON 2. This Kyrie is best sung by a choir, offering the request for forgiveness on behalf of the whole congregation.

KYRIE ELEISON 3. Slightly more sophisticated than *Kyrie eleison 1,* yet it can also be taught to a congregation in four parts. The melody line is extremely simple and requires undergirding harmony. It is best sung at least three times in succession at one specific point in the prayer of confession, preferably before the words of forgiveness are addressed to the congregation.

O LORD, OUR GOD *(Yu Tuhanku).* This is an Indonesian Kyrie which is extremely simple in tune and arrangement. It can be used either to intersperse petitions or before the words of absolution.

Other similar songs
(See page 95 for more information on the following publications.)
Senhor tempiedade de nos (Brazil) – *Many and Great*
Kyrie eleison (Ghana) – *Many and Great*
Agios o Theos (Russia) – *Many and Great*
Kyrie eleison (Russia) – *Many and Great*
Kyrie eleison (Greece) – *Sent by the Lord*
Ch'iu Chu lienmin women (Taiwan) – *Sent by the Lord*

Jesus Christ, Son of God

Words: trad. liturgical

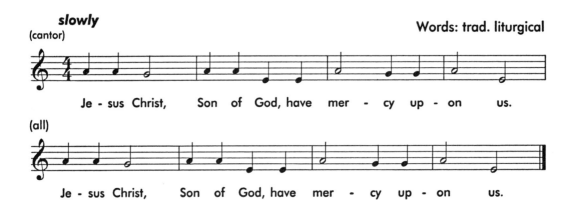

slowly
(cantor)

Je - sus Christ, Son of God, have mer - cy up - on us.

(all)

Je - sus Christ, Son of God, have mer - cy up - on us.

Jesus Christ, Son of God,
have mercy upon us.

alternative

Je - sus Christ, Son of__ God, have mer - cy up - on us.

Kyrie eleison 1

Words: trad. liturgical

Kyrie eleison   (Lord, have mercy)

Kyrie eleison 2

mysteriously

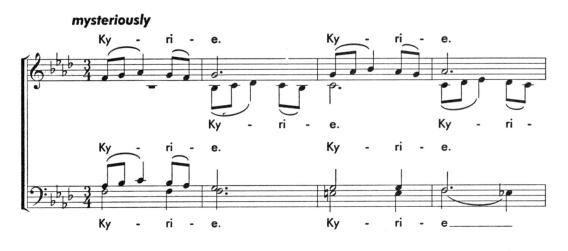

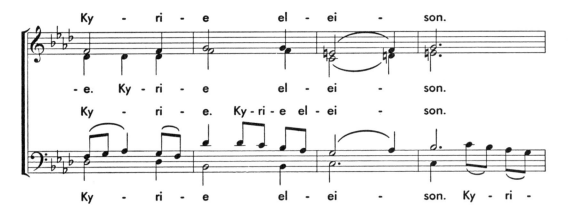

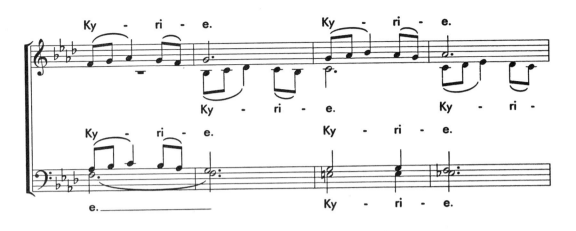

Kyrie eleison   (Lord, have mercy)

Kyrie eleison 3

Ky - ri-e el - ei - son, Chri - ste el - ei - son,

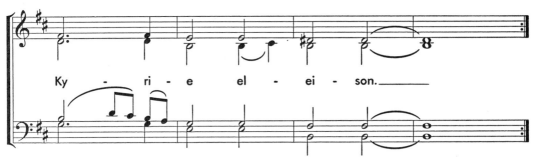

Ky - ri - e el - ei - son.

Kyrie eleison,   (Lord have mercy,
Christe eleison,   Christ have mercy,
Kyrie eleison.   Lord have mercy.)

O Lord, our God (Ya Tuhanku)

Words: ancient liturgical text
Music: Javanese melody amended by Sutarno

calmly

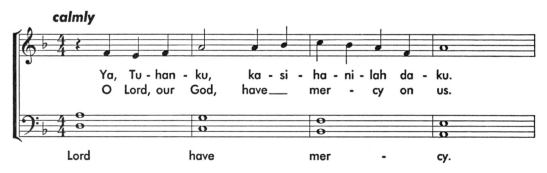

Ya, Tu - han - ku, ka - si - ha - ni - lah da - ku.
O Lord, our God, have___ mer - cy on us.

Lord have mer - cy.

Ya, Tu - han - ku, ka - si - ha - ni - lah da - ku.
O Lord, our God, have___ mer - cy on us.

Lord, have mer - cy.

Ya, Tuhanku, kasihanilah daku.

O Lord, our God, have mercy on us.

ACCLAMATION

There are numerous occasions in life when people make predictable but spontaneous expressions when something good happens. Supporters do it when their team scores a goal; a student may do it when she discovers that she has passed the exam she was sure she had failed; a child does it when his mother surprises him with the news of a forthcoming treat. Often people may say 'Hurray!' or 'Wow!' and such things are said out of joy at the news, the surprise, the realization.

We don't use these specific expressions in worship as a regular part of the liturgy, but we do, or can, sing the *Gloria*. This is an ancient hymn based on the model of the psalms and incorporating the acclamation sung by the angels above the shepherds after announcing Christ's birth.

In some traditions, the full text of the ancient hymn is sung. But most people will be familiar with the abbreviated:

Glory to God in the highest

with or without the additional line:

and on earth peace to those on whom God's favour rests.

The time and place when these words are used in worship vary from tradition to tradition. Some use the *Gloria* to conclude the celebration of Holy Communion; many more will use it to follow the declaration of God's forgiveness or to precede and/or follow the reading of scripture.

GLORIA 1. This is an ancient and simple *Gloria*, which is reckoned to come from the Benedictine period on Iona. Legend has it that it was sung back and forward between monks departing on boats and monks remaining on the island at the start of missionary journeys.

The three parts are very easy to teach. The congregation can be divided into three ad lib or the women can be split into two groups to take the upper parts while all the men sing the lowest part.

GLORIA 2. The two parts of this *Gloria* stand on their own and can be sung separately, but they are best used when sung simultaneously by men *('Deo gratias')* and women *('Gloria in excelsis')*. When using them together, start the men singing once or twice on their own, then bring in the women. This setting is ideal as a recessional.

GLORIA 3. This simple *Gloria* is more of a doxology, praising the three persons in the Trinity. It can be used appropriately after the reading of God's word or after the sermon. It may also be used to intersperse sentences in a prayer of thanksgiving.

The two parts imitate each other and, to this end, the congregation should be divided in two along geographical rather than gender lines.

Other similar songs
(See page 95 for more information on the following publications.)
Gloria (Argentina) – *Many and Great*
Gloria (Peru) – *Sent by the Lord*

Gloria 1

Words: trad. liturgical
Music: traditional

solemnly

Glo - ri - a,   Glo - ri - a,   Glo - ri - a,   in ex - cel - sis De - o.

Not copyright (in the public domain)

Gloria 2

Words: trad. liturgical

brightly

Glo - ri - a   in ex - cel - sis,   Glo - ri - a   in ex - cel - sis,

De - o   gra - ti - as,   De - o   gra - ti - as.

Glo - ri - a, glo - ri - a, glo - ri - a, glo - ri - a, in__ ex - cel - sis De - o.

De - o,__ De - o,__ De - o,__ De - o,__ gra - ti - as De - o.

Gloria in excelsis Deo   Glory to God in the highest.
(Deo gratias)   (Thanks be to God)

Gloria 3

brightly

Glo - ry to God; Praise to the Son;

Glo - ry to God; Praise to the

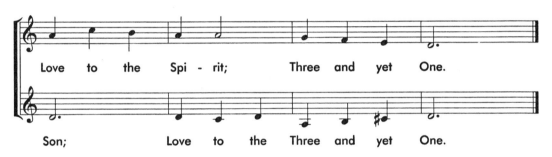

Love to the Spi - rit; Three and yet One.

Son; Love to the Three and yet One.

Glory to God;
Praise to the Son;
Love to the Spirit:
Three and yet One.

THE WORD OF GOD

Christians, like Jews, are people of the Book. We believe that God's communication with humanity has been faithfully interpreted and recorded in the holy scriptures. But, more than that, we believe that the Word of God, present in God's person from the beginning, became seen and known in Jesus, whose words and actions are recorded in the gospels.

Different denominations have a variety of traditions regarding how the Word of God is read in worship. Some require the people to stand as the Bible is brought into the church. Some require people to stand specifically for the reading of the gospel. Some have the scriptures processed into church during a repetitive song, others have the reading of scriptures followed by a sung acclamation. Others yet will have the gospel read not from the lectern, but by the priest or lector standing in the midst of the assembly, flanked by candles and surrounded by incense.

All these traditions and practices underline the importance of the Word of God for Christians, and it may be that this brief perusal may encourage people to feel for how the scriptures might be treated with greater reverence.

The material which follows has a very flexible use. It is nearly all linked to experiences in the life of Jesus and, for that reason, may be particularly associated with the gospel reading. It can equally be used to reflect the seasons of the Christian year or as an aid to meditation.

SEND OUT YOUR LIGHT takes as its text a verse from Psalm 43. It is appropriate for any reading of scripture, but has a particular poignancy during Advent, the time in which we look forward to the Word becoming flesh.

It may be sung as a simple introit on the four Sundays in Advent, or to precede and follow the scripture readings. It may be sung at the beginning of worship as candles are lit and, equally, may be effective at the conclusion of worship as candles are doused and a light precedes the congregation to the exit door. The song suits unaccompanied four-part singing very well, the volume naturally rising and falling in the second and third phrases.

DEUS DE DEO is a phrase taken from the Latin version of the Nicene Creed. It celebrates Christ as God from God, Light from Light. In this context, it may have exactly the same uses as *Send out your light* above. However, as it is in a very simple cantor-and-response style, the whole congregation can quickly be engaged by simply repeating the cantor's line and holding the final note in each phrase.

An alternative – usable with some other material in this section – would be to devise a litany which used different titles or phrases to describe Jesus. Such a litany could act as a meditative prayer after the reading of the gospel and it need not be a set piece. With a little encouragement, it is the kind of activity with which people may join in, adding a phrase spontaneously, after which the verse is sung by way of response.

Examples:

Word of God, one with the Father
Deus de Deo, Lumen de Lumine.
Son of Mary, flesh of our flesh
Deus de Deo...
Carpenter of Nazareth, yoke and table maker
Deus de Deo...
Revealer of God's truth, storyteller and listener
Deus de Deo...
Healer of the sick, toucher of the untouchable
Deus de Deo...
Confronter of the powerful, defender of the poor
Deus de Deo...
Friend of sinners, guest at any table
Deus de Deo...
Victim of slander, silent defendant
Deus de Deo...

Lamb to the slaughter, Saviour of the world

Deus de Deo…

Tenant of a borrowed grave

Deus de Deo…

Voice in a graveyard, resurrected Redeemer

Deus de Deo…

High King of heaven and Lord of our hearts

Deus de Deo…

WORD OF THE FATHER provides a ready-made litany in song. Here a variety of names associated with Jesus are sung by a cantor with the congregation responding, 'Come, Lord, come and take our fear away'.

This may be particularly suited to a service of healing or may be used as an introit at a funeral service. Or again, it may be used to precede the reading of the gospel if, on a particular occasion, the passage celebrates Christ as the one who took away fear, guilt and pain.

VENI IMMANUEL is a particular Advent plea – 'O come, Immanuel' – and, as such, is best used during that season. There is something very appropriate in worship if we only sing certain songs or responses at certain times. It heightens the season and makes clear that these weeks are different from all others. *Veni Immanuel* is not a simple congregational song. It is best sung by a choir, though on one occasion in Salisbury Cathedral, 200 people used it as a recessional while they walked through the choir and nave, singing in perfect harmony.

I AM THE VINE comes from a longer song which paraphrases verses in John's Gospel regarding the dependence of Jesus' disciples on their Lord. That makes these words worth singing on Sundays when baptism or confirmation is celebrated, or on other occasions when there is a focus on discipleship.

It may also be sung as a response breaking up the reading of verses from John 15 thus:

I am the vine…

Verses 1-2

I am the vine…

Verses 3-4

I am the vine…

Verses 5-6

I am the vine…

Verses 7-10

I am the vine…

BEHOLD THE LAMB OF GOD is frequently taken to be a phrase used with regard to the crucifixion. In fact, it appears at the beginning of Christ's ministry. These words, as recorded in John 1 are spoken by John the Baptist to point to Jesus who, at that time, was doing nothing more than walking along a river bank.

The first setting is extremely simple and can be taught to a congregation in four parts. There is only one musical phrase, which is repeated, and none of the parts is beyond the reach of most women and men.

The verse may be appropriate for the Sunday on which the baptism of Jesus is recounted. But like *Deus de Deo* above, it can also be used during a litany celebrating the life of Christ. In some churches it has been successfully used during the administration of Holy Communion.

Another possibility which builds on the litany idea is to allow this verse to be used as an aid to meditation on Jesus' life. With everyone sitting close together, the assembly may be asked to close their eyes and feel for how Jesus is depicted in scripture. Then in random fashion, people say a line or two about how they envisage Jesus, each contribution being followed by the response. A skilful leader will have his or her own contribution to begin and end the meditation.

Examples:

Behold the Lamb of God…

I see Jesus sitting among a crowd of hungry people and asking his disciples, 'What do you have to help feed them?'

Behold the Lamb of God…

I see Jesus astonishing a whole congregation by looking at a sick man in the back corner of the church and asking him to come to the centre and be touched and healed.

Behold the Lamb of God…

I see Jesus in the middle of a group of middle-aged male critics, all anxious to catch him out. Into the circle a little girl – a toddler – walks. He puts his hand on her head and says to his audience, 'Unless you become like this little one, you won't enter the kingdom of heaven.'

Behold the Lamb of God...

And so on.

BEHOLD THE LAMB OF GOD 2. This is a slightly more sophisticated setting of the text, but it is as easy to teach and sing. The soprano and tenor lines are sung in canon. The alto and bass lines have only a repeated four-note phrase with the Latin words *Agnus Dei qui tollis peccata mundi,* which is the Latin equivalent of the English text. The fifth time the notes are sung, the words *Miserere nobis* (have mercy on us) allow the verse to be used as a penitential prayer as much as a response for use during a meditation.

The ease with which this is sung can be gauged from the fact that at an Easter Vigil, broadcast live from Iona Abbey all over Europe in 1993, the congregation who had never heard the song before, learned it 30 minutes before the broadcast, in four parts and without music. When it came the time for the verse to be used during worship, it was meant to be sung once only between portions of scripture. The choir, which had rehearsed the chant, stopped after the first singing; the congregation continued for another singing, without conductor and without flinching!

WONDER AND STARE, like *I am the vine,* is very appropriate for use when a longish portion of scripture is being broken into parts, sometimes with different voices taking different verses.

The tone of the words makes it clear that the verse has specific reference to the final approach to Jerusalem and the Way of the Cross. It has been used sometimes to intersperse readings which indicate how, prior to Palm Sunday, the writing was on the wall. For instance:

Matthew 16.24-28
Matthew 19.27-30
Matthew 20.17-19
Matthew 20.25-28
Matthew 21.1-5

It has also been used effectively as a processional song during the devotional exercise known as the Stations of the Cross. The verse is simply sung as often as is required to enable worshippers to move from one station or venue to another.

More poignantly, it may be used to intersperse the reading of the 'Seven Words' or statements the Gospel writers record being uttered by Jesus on the cross.

AGNUS DEI is the classical text from the Roman Mass which is translated in English 'O Lamb of God, who takes away the sin of the world, have mercy upon us'.

It may be used during prayers of confession as the *Kyrie* is, or it may have a distinctive value if used on Good Friday as people gather to meditate on the cross.

In the course of the celebration of Holy Communion, the *Agnus Dei* is usually sung after the consecration and before the congregation receives.

ALLELUIA 1. Alleluia is not a New Testament word, although it is most commonly associated in worship with the proclamation of the Resurrection or with the sound of angel choirs in heaven.

Alleluia is an exclamation which we find all through the Psalms, a spontaneous uttering of praise to God. It is, of course, appropriate to sing it on Easter Day when the Resurrection is celebrated and, for that reason, many churches do not use it during the penitential seasons of Lent and Advent.

Whether or not that practice is followed, the singing of an Alleluia is an appropriate response to the reading of the gospel, God's good news.

This first Alleluia has a slightly irregular rhythm and requires a four-part singing group for best effect.

ALLELUIA 2 comes from Honduras. It is a much more predictable and gentle setting. For that reason it may be best suited to singing in the evenings or when the reason for jubilation is not of a particularly highly charged variety.

As the three upper parts are parallel, they can easily be taught to a congregation without music.

HERE I STAND finds its text not in the gospels, but in the Book of Revelation where Jesus is depicted as the one who comes to our door and waits to be invited in.

The Sunday after Easter, when the appearance to the doubtful Thomas is remembered, is a time when this verse may be used. It is also appropriate during the sacrament of Holy Communion where Christ waits to be received by his disciples in the bread and wine.

The occasion should determine whether the song is sung with gusto or with tenderness.

POUR OUT takes a text mentioned twice in the scriptures. The relatively unknown prophet Joel stated that a day would come when the Spirit of God would come upon his people in a startling way. In Acts 1, we find Joel's words fulfilled at Pentecost.

The verse may therefore be used at Pentecost and on the Sundays after it to precede the scripture or as an introit or recessional. Because of its immediate association with young people, it might also find use on occasions when there is a focus on youth.

Other similar songs
(See page 95 for more information on the following publications.)

Advent
Come, Lord, come quickly – *Heaven shall not Wait*
Magnificat – *Heaven shall not Wait*
Maranatha (Philippines) – *Sent by the Lord*

Christmas
He became poor – *Love from Below*
He came down (Cameroons) – *Many and Great*

Life of Jesus
Occuli nostri – *Enemy of Apathy*
Watch and pray – *Enemy of Apathy*
Ndingen' endumisweni (South Africa) – *Many and Great*

Lent
O Brother Jesus – *Love from Below*
Agios o Theos (Russia) – *Many and Great*
Re ya mathematha (South Africa) – *Sent by the Lord*

Easter
Amen Alleluia (South Africa) – *Many and Great*
Amen siakudumisa (South Africa) – *Many and Great*
Alleluia (South Africa) – *Sent by the Lord*

Pentecost
Wa wa wa Emimimo (Nigeria) – *Many and Great*

Send out your light

Words: Ps 43.3

quietly but firmly

Send out your light, Lord, send your truth to be my guide.

Then let them lead__ me to__ the place where you__ re - side.

Send out your light, Lord, send your truth
to be my guide.
Then let them lead me to the place
where you reside.

Deus de Deo

Words: trad. liturgical

Deus de Deo,
Lumen de Lumine.

(God from God,
Light from Light.)

Word of the Father

1. Word of the Father,
   Come, Lord, come;
   and take our fear away,
   and take our fear away;
   replace it with your love.

2. Firstborn of Mary,

3. Healer and helper,

4. Servant and sufferer,

5. Jesus, redeemer,

6. Christ resurrected,

7. Maranatha!

Veni Immanuel

Words: trad. liturgical

Veni, veni Immanuel.   (O come, O come, Immanuel.)

I am the vine

Words: Jn 15.5

I am the vine and you the branches,
prun'd and prepar'd for all to see,
chosen to bear the fruit of heaven
if you remain and trust in me.

Behold the Lamb of God 1

Words: Jn 1.29

Behold the Lamb of God, behold the Lamb of God.
He takes away the sin, the sin of the world.

Behold the Lamb of God 2

Words: Jn 1.29

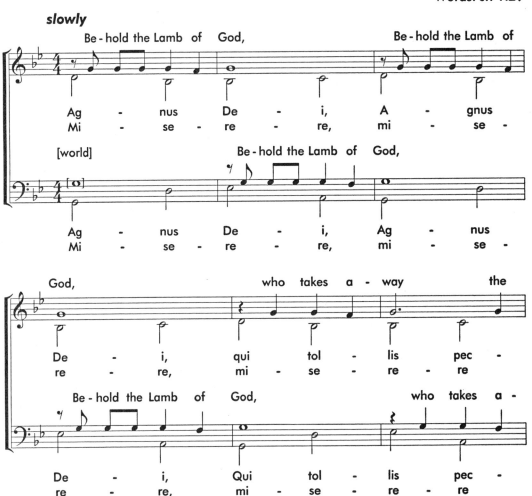

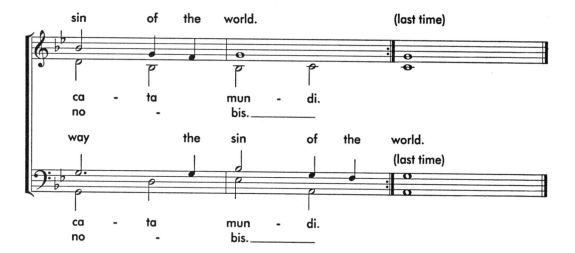

Soprano and tenor

Behold the Lamb of God,
Behold the Lamb of God
who takes away the sin of the world.

Alto and bass

Agnus Dei, Agnus Dei,
qui tollis peccata mundi.

Miserere, miserere,
miserere nobis.

Wonder and stare

mysteriously

Won - der and stare, fear and be - ware,____ Hea - ven and
Hell are close at hand. God's liv - ing Word, Je - sus the
Lord,____ fol - lows where faith and love de - mand.

Wonder and stare, fear and beware,
Heaven and Hell are close at hand.
God's living Word, Jesus the Lord,
follows where faith and love demand.

Agnus Dei

Words: trad. liturgical

quietly but firmly

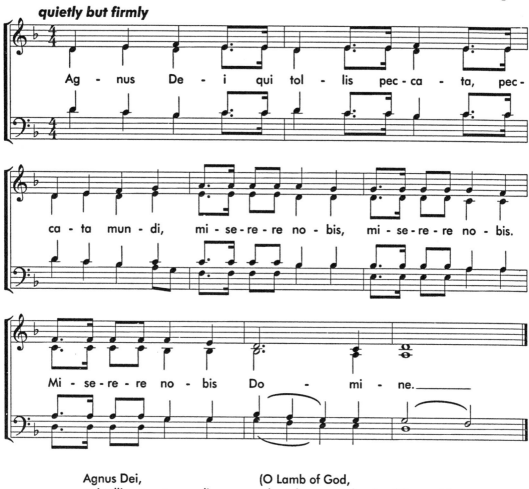

Ag - nus De - i qui tol - lis pec - ca - ta, pec - ca - ta mun - di, mi - se - re - re no - bis, mi - se - re - re no - bis. Mi - se - re - re no - bis Do - mi - ne.____

Agnus Dei,
qui tollis peccata mundi,
miserere nobis, Domine.

(O Lamb of God,
who takes away the sin of the world,
have mercy on us, Lord.)

Alleluia 1

Al - le - lu - ia! Al - le - lu - ia!___ Al - le - lu - ia! Al - le - lu - ia!___

Al - le - lu - ia! Al - le - lu - ia!___ Al - le - lu - ia! Al - le - lu - ia!___

Alleluia!

Alleluia 2

Tune: from Honduras
Arrangement: JLB

Alleluia. Alleluia.
Alleluia. Alleluia.
Alleluia. Alleluia.
El Senōr resucito.

Alleluia (etc.)
Now the Lord is ris'n indeed.

alternative:
Alleluia ...
Glory, love and praise to God.

Here I stand

Words: Rev 3.20

Here I stand at the door and knock, and knock.
I will come and dine
with those who ask me in.

Pour out, I will pour out

Words: Joel 2.28

Pour out, I will pour out my spirit,
Earth shall be more than it seems.
Both sons and daughters shall prophecy,
young and old shall dream dreams.

CONCERN

One of the most selfless things anyone can do is to pray for others. It can happen in absolute secrecy. No credit will be given; it may seem, for all the world, like wasting time. Yet it is what God expects.

How intercessory prayer works is a mystery. There is no direct cause and effect. But when we pray for others we stand, as it were, beside them in solidarity with their pain or their expectation. And in doing so, we make clear to God what are the priorities of our compassion.

Sometimes public prayers of intercession sound like glorified shopping lists; at other times they become so general and innocuous as to encourage drowsiness. Good intercessions should be focused and act as catalysts so that the people of God may both say Amen to the prayer and be enabled to bring any specific concern they have and associate it with the leader's words.

This section is not called 'intercession' partly because the word is obscure to some and also because the material here may be used in prayers or petitions for ourselves as well as for others.

LORD, TO WHOM SHALL WE GO? The text comes from John 6.68 where Peter responds to Jesus' suggestion that some might want to leave him by avowing his utter dependency.

The simple cantor's line and response may be sung repeatedly as a prelude to prayer or may come after each request. It may equally well be used to preface and follow the reading of the gospel.

The alternative four-part arrangement may also be used.

THROUGH OUR LIVES. Like the previous verse, this can be used to intersperse prayer requests, especially if the request is followed by a silence in which people can add their own prayers aloud or quietly. One of the reasons people do not volunteer quickly to lead prayer and are hesitant to participate is that they imagine they will have to speak continuously for about four minutes.

It is therefore important to work on alternatives that can incorporate everybody. Asking people to add just a name or a phrase can often be a way into more participative prayer. For instance:

LEADER: Let us remember and name before God those we keep in our prayers because they are ill.

(Silence. Names. Sung response.)

LEADER: Let us remember and name before God those who depend on us and on whom we depend daily.

(Silence. Names. Sung response.)

And so on.

The response can be sung in two ways: four-part harmony throughout or a cantor singing the first phrase and all responding 'your Kingdom come'.

LORD, IN YOUR MERCY. Here is a very simple but effective four-part response which may be used in exactly the same way as the previous two songs.

Sadly, the word 'mercy' has lost much of its original meaning. We tend to see it as a response in times of emergency as in the phrase 'pleading for mercy', or we associate it with guilt and the need for forgiveness.

God's mercy is not limited to the negative experiences or extremes of life. It is an all-embracing, all-transforming goodness which we can request to shield our joy as much as deal with our sorrow.

MISERERE NOBIS. This is the Latin text for the words 'have mercy on us'. By the character of the music, it will be evident that this should be used more in conjunction with sorrow and loss than with the more positive experiences of life.

The chant was originally used to intersperse the reading of the Passion narrative (Mark 15) on Good Friday. The words were sung three times between each of the major sections of the story, thus allowing the congregation to respond to the drama of Christ's way to the cross. It is particularly effective to do this when, as in the Roman Catholic practice, the Passion story is read by several voices.

In prayer, the chant can be used as a response to words of confession or when praying for the sick and the dying known to the congregation.

DONA NOBIS PACEM IN TERRA. There are some who attribute phenomena such as the de-escalation of the arms race to the diligence and diplomacy of politicians. There is also a divine dimension which operates in and through political people and processes and the urgent prayer of the Church for peace in the world has an incalculable potency. We simply do not know what the world would be like if Christians did not pray for it.

In using *Dona nobis,* it may be sufficient to select four or five items from the world news dealing with situations of violence and war. These need be no more than two sentences long. They will be used to focus prayer, not to broadcast news. When the congregation has been called to prayer and told what is going to happen, people in different parts of the assembly read a passage and may either move immediately into reflective silence or may end with the asking of a question to which people can respond aloud if they so wish. Then the response is sung. For instance:

It was reported yesterday that another successful arms fair was held at Farnborough. The Government is offering substantial trade incentives to developing nations ordering the latest air-to-ground missiles.

What do we ask of God with regard to arms sales?

(Silence or short spoken requests)

Dona nobis...

LISTEN LORD. The text forms the chorus of a song by the same title published in *Heaven shall not Wait.* It refers to how God interprets the groaning of our spirits as well as listening to our crafted prayers. It can be used when prayers focus on aspects of life where it is difficult to know what to pray, and it may be more important to hold our confusion or sense of helplessness before God in terms such as the following:

Let us lay before God our concern and confusion over any known to us who have been the victims or the perpetrators of child abuse.

(Silence. No words. Sung response.)

Let us lay before God our outrage, our anger or our helplessness as we remember those affected by the trade and misuse of drugs in our community.

(Silence. No words. Sung response.)

DON'T BE AFRAID. At a recent Greenbelt Festival, a woman approached one of our Group and said, 'I was here last year, when you taught *Don't be afraid.* At that time I was pregnant. Soon after I had my baby, I went into a severe postnatal depression and had to go into a psychiatric hospital. All through that time, one of the things that kept me going was singing to myself the words of the song.'

This is a testimony to the effectiveness of this verse as much as a vindication of the value of scriptural words set to music which, far removed from the situation of first singing, can become a resource for personal devotion.

The song was written in the wake of the horrific murder of a young girl which devastated a whole community. It may be used in situations of deep personal or corporate grief where there is no easy answer, just the promise of Jesus who has gone through hell before us.

KUMBAYA. This song has been much maligned, partly because in the 60s and 70s it was overused by Western Christians of a liberal disposition. Its endurance and importance to Third World Christians should encourage us to reinstate it, not as a singalong favourite, but as a prayer song which should be sung soulfully.

In our experience, its best use has been when the minimum of words have interspersed the verses and allowed for a constructive time of silence ended by the appropriate verse. For instance:

LEADER: Remember all those who have tears on their faces today for whatever reason.

(Silence or contributions such as 'Lord, remember Andrew', 'Lord, remember my brother's wife')

CANTOR: Someone's crying, Lord,

ALL: Kumbaya (etc.)

Other similar songs
(See page 95 for more information on the following publications.)
I waited, I waited on the Lord – Heaven shall not Wait
Kindle a flame – Heaven shall not Wait
Lord, draw near – Heaven shall not Wait
With God, all things are possible – Heaven shall not Wait
Stand firm (Cameroons) – Many and Great
Mayenziwe (South Africa) – Many and Great
Your Kingdom come (Russia) – Many and Great
If you believe (Zimbabwe) – Sent by the Lord
On God alone I wait silently – Psalms of Patience, Protest and Praise

Lord, to whom shall we go? 1

Words: Jn 6.68

Lord, to whom shall we go?

Yours are the words of e - ter - nal life.

Lord, to whom shall we go? 2

Lord, to whom shall we go? Yours are the words of e - ter - nal life.

Lord, to whom shall we go?
Yours are the words of eternal life.

Through our lives and by our prayers

Through our lives and by our prayers,
your Kingdom come.

Lord, in your mercy

Words: trad. liturgical

Lord, in your mercy,
hear our prayer.

Miserere nobis

Words: trad. liturgical

solemnly

Mi - se - re - re no - bis, mi - se - re - re

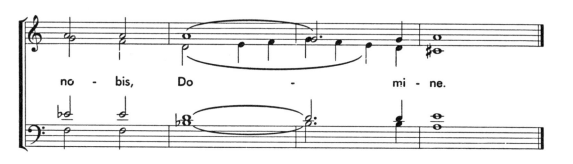

no - bis, Do - mi - ne.

Miserere nobis, Domine.   (Have mercy on us, O Lord.)

Dona nobis pacem in terra

Words: trad. liturgical

Do - na no - bis pa - cem in ter - ra,

do - na no - bis pa - cem, Do - mi - ne.

Dona nobis pacem in terra,
dona nobis pacem, Domine.

Grant us peace on earth,
grant us peace, O Lord.

Listen, Lord

Lis - ten, Lord, lis - ten Lord, not to our words but to our_ prayer._

You a - lone, you a - lone un - der - stand and care.

Listen, Lord, listen, Lord,
not to our words but to our prayer
You alone, you alone
understand and care.

Don't be afraid

Don't be afraid. My love is stronger,
my love is stronger than your fear.
Don't be afraid. My love is stronger
and I have promis'd, promis'd to be always near

Kumbaya

Words & tune: Afro-Caribbean, traditional
Arrangement: JLB

1. Kumbaya, my Lord, Kumbaya (x3)
   O Lord Kumbaya.

2. Someone's crying, Lord, Kumbaya...

3. Someone's dying, Lord, Kumbaya...

4. Someone's shouting, Lord, Kumbaya...

5. Someone's praying, Lord, Kumbaya...

6. Kumbaya, my Lord... (as verse 1)

GRATITUDE

'It is good to give thanks to the Lord' is a recurrent theme in the Psalms, much the same as 'count your blessings' is a recurrent phrase in folk wisdom. There is something valuable in setting against our worries and negative feelings a remembrance of the good things in life, the surprises which have happened, the difficulties which have been overcome and the intrinsic goodness of life itself.

To some people, the corporate expression of gratitude to God – as of praise – brings a sense of awkwardness. The more flamboyant demonstrations of charismatic worship or the questionable sincerity of 'good time/old time' worship makes them reluctant to show too much exuberance lest it be taken the wrong way. Whether or not this is a Western fixation or one more common among Calvinists than Catholics is debatable, but the need to offer warmhearted thanks to God remains. It is hoped that the following verses might allow enthusiasm to bubble up, even amongst the most reticent.

O BLESS THE LORD. Psalm 103 provides the text and the music is set in an Afro–American style. It can be sung in four parts or in two with men taking the bass and women the soprano lines.

The song can be used as an introit to worship, as a recessional, as a response to the reading of the gospel or to intersperse prayers of gratitude where the musical line almost trips over the spoken word. For instance:

LEADER: Let us give thanks to God for this day, this place and everyone around us.

ALL: *(immediately) O bless the Lord...*

LEADER: Let us remember that God knows all our names and calls us by name.

ALL: *O bless the Lord...*

LEADER: Let us rejoice that we can worship freely in this land.

ALL: *O bless the Lord... (etc.)*

Such a pattern may, in some communities, allow for spontaneous contributions encouraging the congregation to sing.

LET THE GIVING OF THANKS. Psalm 50.23 provides this text which, as with *O bless the Lord*, requires some part singing.

Ideally, this should be a song of praise which gradually builds up. There are three main vocal lines and, if the congregation has been subdivided, a cantor who sings part A should sing it once then encourage those in that section to join in. When they are comfortable with the part, the volume should drop while a second cantor introduces part B to the second section. They sing, drop in volume, and the third cantor introduces part C.

This is not so likely to be used to intersperse prayers as to provide a fitting conclusion to a prayer or a whole act of worship.

GLORY AND GRATITUDE AND PRAISE. Like *Let the giving of thanks*, this is more a song for concluding an act of worship or a section within the liturgy than for responding to phrases of prayer. It also has the benefit of being teachable in a similar way.

Even though the congregation does not have the music, they can be divided into high and low women, high and low men, and learn the appropriate parts, building the song up as in the previous item.

Because the bass has a minimal vocal line and the upper parts have a parallel progression, it is easily picked up even by the least enthusiastic.

Other similar songs
(See page 95 for more information on the following publications.)
Imela (Nigeria) – *Many and Great*
Bayuvaya (South Africa) – *Sent by the Lord*

O bless the Lord

Words: Ps 103.2

brightly

O my soul, O my

O bless the Lord,_____ O bless the Lord,_____

soul, bless the Lord and ne - ver for - get his

O bless the Lord, bless the Lord and ne - ver for - get his

love!   O   my   soul,   O   my

love!   O   bless   the   Lord,_____   O   bless   the   Lord,_____

soul,   bless   the   Lord   and   ne - ver for - get   his   love!

—   O, bless the   Lord, bless   the   Lord   and   ne - ver for - get   his   love!

O bless the Lord O my soul,
and never forget his love!

Let the giving of thanks

Words: Ps 50.23

very relaxed

Let the giv - ing of thanks___ be our sac - ri - fice___ to

God. Let the giv - ing of thanks___ be our

sac - ri - fice___ to God. (descant optional) Let the giv - ing of thanks___

Let the giv - ing of thanks___

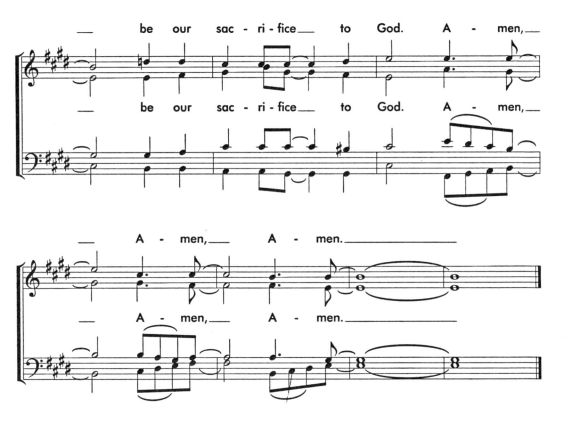

Let the giving of thanks be our sacrifice to God. Amen.

Glory and gratitude and praise

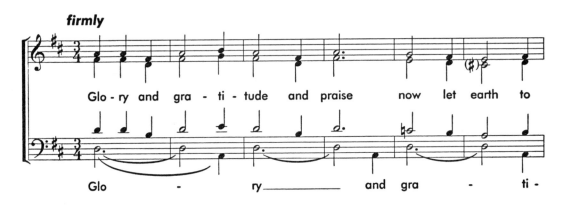

Glo-ry and gra-ti-tude and praise now let earth to

Glo - ry and gra - ti -

hea-ven raise. Glo-ry and gra-ti-tude and praise:

- tude and praise

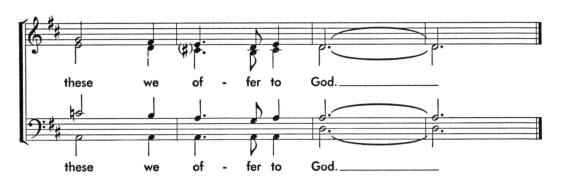

these   we   of - fer to   God.

these   we   of - fer to   God.

Glory and gratitude and praise
now let earth to heaven raise.
Glory and gratitude and praise:
these we offer to God.

LEAVING

As with gathering, there is a tendency among British Christians to assume that a church service cannot end unless there has been some kind of organ voluntary or instrumental play-out, even though few people remain to listen to the music.

While there are many situations where this will be the case, it need not always be so. There is something very affirmative about moving from the sanctuary into the street in song, or about feeling that the voice of the people can have – from time to time – the last word, after which no more music is required.

In previous sections, especially Acclamation, items were listed which can be sung as recessionals. The Alleluias in the Word of God section can also be used this way.

It will be apparent that the songs in this section are not all lively recessional ones.

BEHOLD, I MAKE ALL THINGS NEW. As with *Take O take me as I am* (below) this song may be used to conclude worship in which there has been a focus on personal dedication and commitment. It can be sung on the move, and is especially enjoyable if the two main parts have been learned according to gender.

These two parts imitate each other and once people have sung them through once, they tend to stick in the mind. There is a third part, written tongue in cheek, for people who say they can only sing two notes. Calling on those who want to sing in a monotone, the leader should teach this by stretching one hand out in front and dipping it as the note drops from G to F sharp at the end of each musical phrase.

FOR YOURS IS THE KINGDOM. This may be sung repeatedly at the end of the Lord's Prayer, or it might be sung at the end of a prayer of commitment or as a form of benediction when the last spoken phrase naturally leads into the song. For instance:

> ...so we give all that we have and are to you, with no fear or reservation
>
> *For yours is the Kingdom ...*

or:

> ...into your safekeeping we commit ourselves, O God, this night and every night
>
> *For your is the Kingdom ...*

The song is particularly effective if, in the initial singings, it moves quietly and gently, gradually building up in volume and intensity.

TAKE O TAKE ME AS I AM. This verse is primarily a quiet song of dedication. It may be used as people walk forward to the front of the sanctuary during an act of commitment; it may be used when people have been confirmed or it may simply be used to offer ourselves to God at the end of an act of worship or some intentional gathering.

If people find the key of D flat major awkward to read, or should the music be arranged for strings, change the five flats into two sharps and read it in D major.

AMEN. This is one of the easiest Amens to teach, especially to a British congregation. The music is pentatonic, which is an immediate help in assimilating the melody. It also falls naturally into a four-part canon. After singing it through three times in unison, an assembly can be directed to break into parts and sing it in canon as the church is vacated. There is no problem if someone forgets the line. He or she simply needs to wait for two bars and start again from the beginning with another 25% of the congregation.

Other similar songs
(See page 95 for more information on the following publications.)
Halle, halle, halle (Caribbean) – *Many and Great*
Wen Ti (China) – *Sent by the Lord*
Sent by the Lord (Nicaragua) – *Sent by the Lord*

Behold, I make all things new

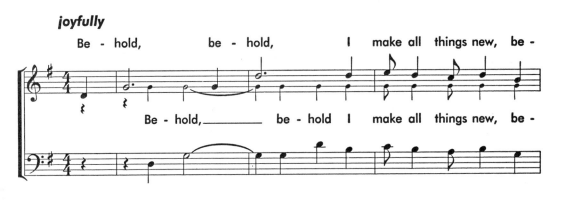

joyfully

Be - hold, be - hold, I make all things new, be -

Be - hold, be - hold I make all things new, be -

gin - ning with you and start - ing from to - day. Be -

gin - ning with you and start - ing from to - day.

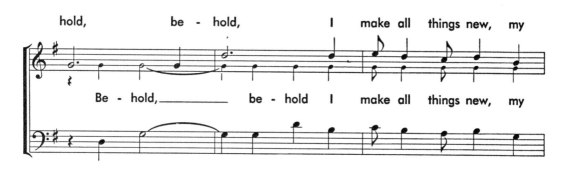

hold, be - hold, I make all things new, my

Be - hold,_____ be - hold I make all things new, my

pro - mise is true, for I am Christ the way.

pro - mise is true, for___ I am Christ the way.

Behold, behold I make all things new,
beginning with you
and starting from today.
Behold, behold I make all things new,
my promise is true,
for I am Christ the way.

For yours is the Kingdom

Words: trad. liturgical

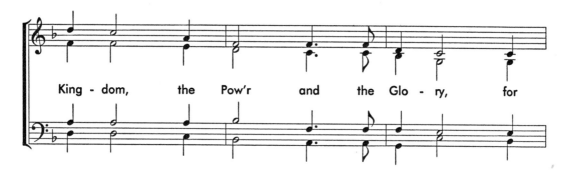

King - dom,   the   Pow'r   and   the   Glo - ry,   for

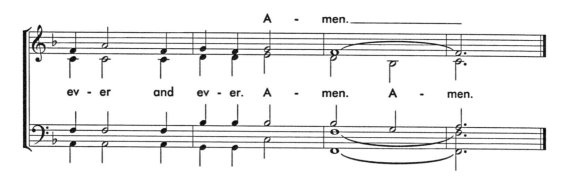

ev - er   and   ev - er. A - men.   A - men.

A - men.

For yours is the Kingdom, the Power and the Glory,
for ever and ever. Amen.

Take, O take me as I am

Take, O take me as I am; summon out what I shall be; set your seal upon my heart and live in me.

Take, O take me as I am;
summon out what I shall be;
set your seal upon my heart
and live in me.

Amen

lively tempo

Amen, amen, alleluia, amen.

A COMMUNION SETTING

The St Bride setting of the *Kyrie* (Lord have mercy), *Sanctus* (Holy, Holy), *Benedictus* (Blessed is the one) and *Agnus Dei* (Lamb of God) is offered for use at celebrations of Holy Communion where – for reasons of necessity or design – there is neither choir nor organ. All that is required is a cantor and the absolute minimum of rehearsal time. The *Kyrie* was taught to a crowd of 20,000 in under half-a-minute!

KYRIE. Take very slowly and deliberately, with as much tenderness or urgency in the cantor's singing as the situation requires. The congregation simply hums in response to the first two phrases and sings the *eleison* after the third. If a large drum (bass, tom or bodhran) is available, it can add urgency by beating as indicated while the congregation hums.

SANCTUS AND BENEDICTUS. Sing with liveliness, the congregation imitating each phrase exactly, though the entries for the second and fourth phrases are irregular. The *Sanctus* should be sung twice and the coda at the *Benedictus* should increase in volume.

AGNUS DEI. A gentle and quiet piece in distinction from the above. If desired, it can be sung as a four-part canon at the bar.

Kyrie eleison (St Bride setting)

Words: trad. liturgical

Kyrie eleison.   (Lord have mercy,
Christe eleison.   Christ have mercy,
Kyrie eleison.   Lord have mercy.)

Sanctus and Benedictus (St Bride setting)

Words: trad. liturgical

Holy, Holy, Holy Lord,
God of power and might,
Heaven and earth are full of your glory.

Blessed is the one who comes
in the name of the Lord!
Hosanna in the highest!

Agnus Dei (St Bride setting)

Words: trad. liturgical

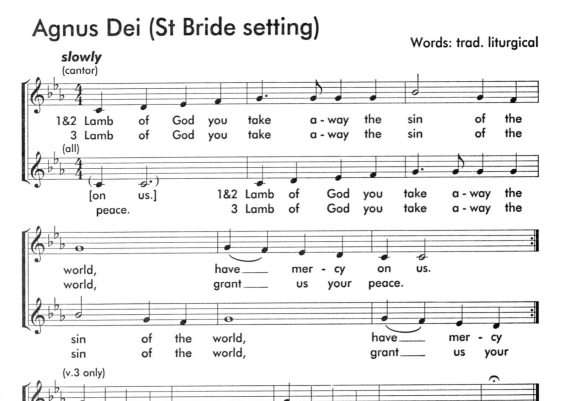

slowly

1&2 Lamb of God you take a-way the sin of the
3 Lamb of God you take a-way the sin of the

[on us.] 1&2 Lamb of God you take a-way the
peace. 3 Lamb of God you take a-way the

world, have____ mer - cy on us.
world, grant____ us your peace.

sin of the world, have____ mer - cy
sin of the world, grant____ us your

(v.3 only)
Grant__ us your peace. Grant__ us your peace._____

(v.3 only)
peace. Grant__ us your peace. Grant__ us your peace.

Lamb of God you take away the sin of the world,
have mercy on us.
Lamb of God you take away the sin of the world,
Grant us your peace.

94   Music © 1995 The Iona Community. GIA Publications, Inc. exclusive North American agent.

OTHER WORSHIP RESOURCES
FROM THE WILD GOOSE WORSHIP GROUP

Songbooks*

Enemy of Apathy (Wild Goose Songs Vol. 2) 1988 John L Bell & G Maule
Heaven shall not Wait (Wild Goose Songs Vol. 1)1988 J L Bell & G Maule
Innkeepers and Light Sleepers (Seventeen new songs for Christmas) 1992 J L
    Bell
Love from Below (Wild Goose Songs Vol. 3)1989 J L Bell & G Maule
Many and Great (Songs of the World Church Vol. 1) 1990 J L Bell (ed./arr.)
Psalms of Patience, Protest and Praise 1993 J L Bell
Sent by the Lord (Songs of the World Church Vol. 2)1991 J L Bell (ed./arr.)

Recordings by the Wild Goose Worship Group*

Cloth for the Cradle (cassette)
Come all you People (cassette)
Heaven shall not Wait (cassette)
Innkeepers and Light Sleepers (cassette)
Love from Below (cassette)
Many and Great (cassette)
Psalms of Patience, Protest and Praise (cassette and CD)
Sent by the Lord (cassette)
A Touching Place (cassette)

Other resources*

He was in the World (Meditations for public worship) 1995 J L Bell

INDEX